OWL OF
MINERVA

ALSO BY ERIC PANKEY

For the New Year
Heartwood
Apocrypha
The Late Romances
Cenotaph
Oracle Figures
Reliquaries
The Pear as One Example: New and Selected Poems
Trace
Dismantling the Angel
Crow-Work
Augury

OWL OF MINERVA

POEMS BY **ERIC PANKEY**

MILKWEED EDITIONS

Published 2019 by Milkweed Editions
Printed in the United States of America
Cover design by Mary Austin Speaker
Cover illustration by Mary Austin Speaker
19 20 21 22 23 5 4 3 2 1
First Edition

Milkweed Editions, an independent nonprofit publisher, gratefully acknowledges sustaining support from the Alan B. Slifka Foundation and its president, Riva Ariella Ritvo-Slifka; the Ballard Spahr Foundation; *Copper Nickel*; the Jerome Foundation; the McKnight Foundation; the National Endowment for the Arts; the National Poetry Series; the Target Foundation; and other generous contributions from foundations, corporations, and individuals. Also, this activity is made possible by the voters of Minnesota through a Minnesota State Arts Board Operating Support grant, thanks to a legislative appropriation from the arts and cultural heritage fund. For a full listing of Milkweed Editions supporters, please visit milkweed.org.

Library of Congress Cataloging-in-Publication Data

Names: Pankey, Eric, 1959- author.

Title: Owl of Minerva : poems / Eric Pankey.

Description: First edition. | Minneapolis, Minnesota : Milkweed Editions, 2019.

Identifiers: LCCN 2019008909 (print) | LCCN 2019009535 (ebook) | ISBN 9781571317261 (ebook) | ISBN 9781571315106 (paperback : alk. paper)

Classification: LCC PS3566.A575 (ebook) | LCC PS3566.A575 A6 2019 (print) | DDC 811/.54—dc23

LC record available at https://lccn.loc.gov/2019008909

Milkweed Editions is committed to ecological stewardship. We strive to align our book production practices with this principle, and to reduce the impact of our operations in the environment. We are a member of the Green Press Initiative, a nonprofit coalition of publishers, manufacturers, and authors working to protect the world's endangered forests and conserve natural resources.

for Karlyn, Clare & Jennifer

CONTENTS

I.

THE COMPLETE LIST OF EVERYTHING *(An Excerpt)* 3

II.

THE SET OF THE WHOLE 15
COLD MOUNTAIN 16
THE ENCLOSED FIELD 17
SPELL FOR CALLING DOWN RAIN 18
ONE ENTERS TO FIND THE DIVINE 19
TO KNOCK AT AN EMPTY HOUSE 20
THE WEIGHT OF LIGHT 21
FEVER DREAM 22
DREAM WITH HAN-SHAN 23
THINKING ABOUT THE AFTERLIFE 24

III.

ISLAND REFUGE 27
ICEBERG IN MIST 30
A MAP OF VENICE 31
SEEING THINGS 32
THE VERNACULAR 33
TO CONFIRM THE EARTH'S ROTATION 34
THREE MATHEW BRADY CIVIL WAR PHOTOGRAPHS 36
STUDY FOR "THE DAY OF JUDGMENT" 39
PEMAQUID POINT 40
THE WAPSIPINICON 41

IV.

THE COMPLETE LIST OF EVERYTHING *(Recovered Loose-leaf Pages)* 45

V.

THE LAST SUNDAY IN LENT 51
ANOTHER READING 52
MELANCHOLIA 53
ARCADIAN INSCRIPTIONS 54
PARABLE WITH MY FATHER AS A BOY 55

A PUBLIC EDUCATION   56
MY FATHER AMID THE SHADES   57
BOOK OF HOURS   58
TROUBLE IN MIND   63
THE SIDE EFFECTS OF MIMICRY   64

VI.

THE INTERVENING YEARS   67
LINES AT MIDSUMMER   68
THE ATTENTION AN ENIGMA DEMANDS   69
ELSEWHERE   70
MEDITATION AT RIO DEVA   72
SOJOURN AND TRANSIT   75
IN THE PRESENCE OF ANIMALS   76
A MAP OF THE FRONTIER   78
AS THROUGH A SHEER CURTAIN   79
SOUVENIRS   80

VII.

THE COMPLETE LIST OF EVERYTHING *(An Addendum)*   83

VIII.

THE CONTINUOUS PRESENT   89
ABOVE AT AND JUST BELOW SEA LEVEL   91
DIVINATION BENEATH THUNDER   92
PLAIN SIGHT   93
IN THE EVER-FRESHENED KEYS   95
ALL SHALL BE RESTORED   96
SANCTUARY   100
OWL OF MINERVA   101
DEBRIS OF AN OCTOBER EVENING   102
DREAM TRANSLATION   103

Acknowledgments   105
Notes   109

The great collector is perturbed from
the outset by the dispersion and chaos
that subsume everything in the world.
WALTER BENJAMIN

The feeling that the world is a limited
whole is the mystical feeling.
LUDWIG WITTGENSTEIN

I. II. III. IV. V. VI. VII. VIII.

THE COMPLETE LIST OF EVERYTHING
(An Excerpt)

Plow blade excavated from a tomb
Roof of camphor and cypress
Longbow of lacquered catalpa wood

The error considered a source of lively regret
A folded length of willow-green silk
The moon hidden perhaps

Four rough ink sketches of cicadas
The error considered a serious lapse of taste
Hailstorm over open sea

Perspective box with Dutch interior
The continuum of a pantoum
The tyranny of the present tense

Empty space filled with conjecture
Four angels holding the winds at bay
Whirlpool in a tsunami's wake

Carved bone buttons wax-dipped rose
The red end of the spectrum
The spotted hood of a pitcher plant

Whitetail hung from a barn's crossbeam
Ticktock of blood into a galvanized pail
Nanny goat atop a steaming dung heap

A golden age when Saturn ruled
The error unacknowledged as error
This and this and this and this and this

Thicket of rusted razor wire
Lightning strike interred as glass in sand
Confluence of the Fox and the Wabash

Dead man resuscitated by a single word
Healer with a birdcage for a head
Fragments of a much larger thing

Vipers awake this late in the season
Sooty smoke of a kerosene lantern
No Trespassing sign riddled with buckshot

Cold stove of a peat bog
The least dangerous of reported side effects
Rhyme of *allure* and *terror*

Jesus in the house of Mary and Martha
Fog a fugue of interlocking grays
A nail clipping's sharp ends

Antebellum antecedent antediluvian
Antelope antemortem antenna
Antepenultimate anthem anther anthill

Solidarity undermined by rumor
Charlie Parker's grave in Kansas City
Verb meaning *to look back from the seventh day*

Noun meaning *a discrete body of work*
"Great Speckled Bird" sung by Lucinda Williams
Contradictions common in dreams

Fragment of an Egyptian queen's face in yellow jasper
Abandoned crutches at Chimayo
King Lear Act 4 scene 7 lines 43–46

Redacted version of the torture report
Vague sense of having been here before
The error that unfolds into good fortune

The cellar stairs submerged in flood
Goat-footed Pan tapping a tree for honey
Rhyme of *recur* and *endure*

Below where bodies writhe as flames
Last dregs of a turned and livery port
A poor and jerry-built rebuttal

Smeared stain of a loose saffron thread
Ice-heaved tumble of stone wall
Soul awaiting its body's arrival

Shreds debris tailings shrapnel
Onslaught of grief without apparent occasion
Fall of acorns on a shed's tin roof

Spilt cauldron of a hornet's nest
Hyphen that links and keeps separate
Threshold uncrossed by Eurydice

"The Great Speckled Bird" sung by Roy Acuff
Spanish moss's ghostly webwork
OK meaning *be that as it may*

Pinyon pines wild olives chiffchaffs goldfinches
Inarticulate cries and gestures
The past like a struck string shimmers anew

Screen door caught before it slams
Gleaned windfall all pocked and blemished
A thermometer's acrid trace of alcohol

A string of fine purple wool to bind bay leaves
Trance utterance ecstatic murmur glossolalia
Green shoot from a withered tree

Compendiums and bestiaries
Commentaries on commentaries on commentaries
"Peace in the Valley" sung by Sister Rosetta Tharpe

"Peace in the Valley" sung by Clara Ward and the Clara Ward Singers
"(There'll Be) Peace in the Valley" sung by Loretta Lynn
Thimble cap black morel horsehair mummy-cap

Sky's clear / night's sea / green of the mountain pool /
Cow cress poor-man's-pepper shepherd's purse
Aftershocks along the fault line

Contingency quintessence
Ancient harbor silted in
Nod of moored skiffs in the wake

Cocklebur imported in bales of wool
The five hundred year flood plain
Tumor on my mother's tongue

Pretext by which one begins to speak
Curative waters in glass vials
Falcon mantled over its prey

The translucence of the Eternal through and in the Temporal
Black tacks kept in an old baby food jar
Emery board tweezers eyelash curler

Owl of Minerva nostalgia for the infinite
The forgery authenticated
Cobra black mamba desert death adder

Verb meaning *to forget a dream upon waking*
Bunkers beyond the dunes
Arranged order of an encyclopedia

Periodic table period piece
The quorum the denouement the flimflam
Stubborn door latch sooty ceiling

Gate of ivory gate of horn
A thread bit not cut all fray and snarl
Noun meaning *the first to acknowledge a miracle*

Verb meaning *to build up in order to tear down*
The luck of the draw unfinished business
Split infinitives slipped disc

Inventory of the summer's yield
The Chester-Hadlyme Ferry
A tornado's lash and drag

The error considered tragic
Carp and bluegill in a quarry lake
Woven wool of a Viking sail

Ice-spalled brick face wind-rucked shingles
First word that comes to mind
First in a series of errors foretold

Soluble rock such as limestone dolomite and gypsum
Transom knot tumble hitch slippery eight loop
The nine rasas the ninth planet

Cold fog from which a trawler emerges
Slug loose change foreign coins
Two iambs followed by a spondee

The work and charm of memory
Two whole notes a rest
An outline darkened in with charcoal

Verb meaning *recently departed from a place*
Detour that ends in a dead end
Ram snagged in a thicket

Papyrus fragment with lines from Homer's *Odyssey*
Game of Hounds and Jackals
Warm laundry in a wicker basket

Match crimped and blackened by flame
Spindly taproot of a dream
Bottle tree glottal stop gingko leaf

The dung beetle the stag
Unbleached coarse linen
A body's obedience to gravity

Ritual functions of repetition
Bed of nails a sarcophagus an arcane song
An enclosed interior called *a shelter*

A carton of Camels a cartoon duck
Surveyors' instruments abstracting a field
Sconces niches amphorae

Levee crested not broken
A surface blackened to absorb light
Dugout canoe horse trough pothole

Deputy Dawg singing *Dreadful sorry, Clementine*
The rafters' regimented shadows
An invitation to the voyage

Jabs gouges scars facets
A child's counting game
Ruined chapel collapsed circus tent

Forthcoming revelations
Narrative sustained by *and then*
Ghost pale before a whitewashed wall

Edges rounded by wear
Incunabula incarnadine incandescence
Fertile crescent futile attempt

A wheel in a wheel way in the middle of the air
The unforgiveable error the error of pride
Sporadic killings after a massacre

Circular calendar of megaliths
A colander's functional elegance
A pair of aces three twos

False eyelashes false indigo false start
The *avant-garde's* puritanical zeal
A counterweight an assumed consensus

Moment when theory replaces practice
An unattended tripe cart near Dante's house
The unintended consequences

Mercator projection mercenary mercurochrome
This and that but more of that than this
Verb meaning *to be reminded of a place you've never visited*

A stowaway a splinter a virus
Scarp's erosion wind-riven scarecrow
The error of the sentimental

A random number generator
The pretense of pictorial depth
A Madrid morning's pale silver shimmer

Glass pill bottle Duane Allman used as a slide
Penknife Blind Willie Johnson used as a slide
What de Chirico calls *the metaphysics of the most ordinary objects*

Green door into a courtyard
The background the backbeat the backhand
Shortwave radio left on all night

Child born not from a body but from sleep
Dark energy stone light a journey's tedium
Just the cello's part of a late quartet

The name everyone called her
Verb meaning *to abstract to the edge of recognizability*
Reverie rather than engagement

Shape a dress takes as it falls to the floor
Jar of star anise opened
The mind as a repository

A prairie a pasture edged with oaks
A granite erratic half submerged in a wetland
What occludes what dims resolution

A slur a slub a sluicing
Upriver tributaries flint strike of horse hooves
Grapes left on a gleaned vine

A discourse on love a distillation
What is unknown unknowable
The metaphoric dimension of rhyme

A banked ember words that baffle
Another day older and deeper in debt
Uneven floorboards the blue of Mary's robes

Rigid geometries of a rented room
A chrome bumper's severe gleam and glare
Buttonwood's rubbed-off bark

Angles of rooflines field of shocked corn
Public farm auction outside Lone Tree
Malware warehouse household holdfast

Rough-haired terrier digging for moles
Silky plumage of a crow's wing
Set of six ladder-back chairs for forty dollars

The awaited verdict *chanted snatches of old tunes*
The Connecticut from Deep River to the Sound
Open shutter above Piazza Santo Spirito

"Dark Was the Night, Cold Was the Ground" sung by Blind Willie Johnson
The past authenticated by a souvenir
The finite algorithms of *etcetera*

I . **II.** III . IV . V . VI . VII . VIII .

THE SET OF THE WHOLE

The hope was to construct

A coherent totality of meaning from odds
And ends, to suggest everything without
The burden of chronology, or its boredom—

Each thing equal to the next—*the discord*
Of senses beside *morning temple bell in mist*
Next to *acid-bit copper plate*, to suggest

An infinity without a cluttered dump
At the end of it, to suggest *the whole*
Without having to live the whole of each life.

After all, the past *is* extricable,
Easily categorized, sorted, set on sturdy shelves,
The paper trail neat in accordion files,

The once-animate preserved in wax,
Pinned to Styrofoam, ordered and labeled,
Or afloat in cloudy water and formaldehyde,

And yet what one hopes is to evoke the experience
Of a thing, of things, and not construct or curate
Yet another museum, or fill to the gills

One more storage unit out on the edge of town
Near the payday loans and check-cashing services,
Where much is made out of very little.

COLD MOUNTAIN

Fog lifts from the valley,
                    displaces a mountain:
Fog like the broad white space on a six-fold screen
From which ink is absent.

Here and there:
                    a casual paraphrase of gray
To suggest the fog has substance,
Is substantial, can replace a peak,

Yet appears, nevertheless,
                    a mere surface,
A flat expanse, nothing, really, to notice.
That which is, which was, before: emptiness.

THE ENCLOSED FIELD

The stones, rearranged,
Enclose the field
They once inhabited.

The stones frame, thus
Create, an interior.

The halved moon
Shimmers between
Translucency and opacity.

Time intervenes:
Wind striations on the stones,
An algebra of marks and traces.

Each stone, moonlit,
Is bereft of memory.

A dry stone wall
Surrounds the settled space,
The sheer absence.

SPELL FOR CALLING DOWN RAIN

Unbraid a sooty wick.

Dig down through
An ancient influx of mudflows
To find a riverbed.

Take as a unit of measure
The expanse of a summer afternoon.

Chip out a sliver of a glacier's solemn blue.

For the transit of an instant,
Stand still.

Rain will begin to fall in the foreseeable future.

To initiate an end,
Re-braid the wick.

Touch the oily char
On your index finger to your forehead.

For the transit of an instant,
Stand still.

ONE ENTERS TO FIND THE DIVINE

One enters to find the divine
But encounters instead an afterimage:
The flat harshness of noon,

The airy stuff of milkweed,
Thistle, or poplar, ghostly, aloft.
As one's eyes adjust, the dark

Sorts itself out as smoke or fog,
A cloud in a cloud chamber,
A whiteout riddled with sleet.

Like a bulb's filament,
The compass needle shimmers
Over an italicized capital *N.*

There is no East, no West, no South.
One turns and turns and turns
And cannot breath as the horizon tightens.

TO KNOCK AT AN EMPTY HOUSE

There is no serum for sleep's dusky venom.
The night path's chalk clings to your shoes:
Missteps mapped as you followed the hedge maze

And found at last a threshold's shelter.
Twin doors, like triptych wings, open outward,
Reveal the recurrence of the as-yet-to-happen.

If you consider entering, you have entered
And wonder at the wisdom of entering.
Such disarray. A stage set *to suggest disarray.*

THE WEIGHT OF LIGHT

Like a story distorted by retelling,
These days, seemingly the same, appear
As if new, versions, perhaps, of a yesterday—
Elongated, bent, or collapsed, off-kilter—
Alive with the alterity of enigma,
And make the spectral tangible, the opaque
See-through-able. On such a day affection
Is contagious, and tomorrow, just a matter of time.
Memory stains, is a stain, but rarely indelible.
Often stripped of our bearings, we consider
How this place reminds us of that one:
Daylight blue on the face of a glacier,
The chameleon attribute of air in Santa Fe,
The edges sharply focused at that altitude.
So much to be noticed after the fact, retroactively,
That to live in the present tense demands a flexibility,
A dexterity we have not brought to the occasion.
Even here with you, sheltered from the lightning,
The finery and furnishings of storm, I feel
The past spreading behind us as a dragnet.
It sinks into the increasing darkness of depths,
Grows heavy and never will be hauled back up.
I can hardly remember the day before yesterday:
No wind. The weight of light moved
An untorn web between two dogwoods
Until motion and stillness concurred.
Then the single notch of a second hand's gear,
A drawn breath. On what scale, with what increment
Do we begin to measure the substantial?

FEVER DREAM

In the clearing he is surrounded by trees.
Slow wind. One sound: the icy cogs
Catching as snow gathers on snow.
He imagines a bed of pine needles
Upon which he might give in to sleep.
His hands are not cold. Each burns
As if he carried embers in his fists.
Perhaps a horse will trudge the distance,
Find him, lead him back through the trees.
Perhaps this shallow meadow was a pond once,
And where he stands he is in over his head.
He looks up, sees overhead the shadowed underside
Of a boat slow, then stall, as ice seizes its sides.

DREAM WITH HAN-SHAN

The gray sky still holds chisel marks
And floats as stone above quarry depths.
The path out switchbacks: a jagged meander.
He empties his knapsack,
                            stacks five stones into a cairn.
In sequence they reenact the excavation's history.
Where the path meets the road, fog burns off.
He can see just how far it is to anywhere.

THINKING ABOUT THE AFTERLIFE
for Charles Wright

Pine island behind a façade of fog;
A fish crow caws as it flies.

Blueberries on their way to ripe,
Greenish, not yet glaucous.

I give up on infinity,
Court the end of things:

In the sweet by-and-by,
We shall meet on that beautiful shore;

In the sweet by-and-by,
We shall meet on that beautiful shore.

I.II.**III.**IV.V.VI.VII.VIII.

ISLAND REFUGE
for Peggy Yocom and John Slack

The task is simple:
Sustain the moment a moment longer,

Or in the moment
Attend more wholly,

Keenly focused on the quotidian,
Which is all there is,

And out of which the metaphysical is spun.
We hiked one of the forty-three islands of the archipelago

Through stands of coastal jack pine
(Twisted, stunted, hardy,

Adapted to reproduce in the absence of fire)
To the island's exposed headlands,

Or rather, almost, to where we lost the trail,
Tired, and retraced our steps

Back over raised bogs
(Thousands of years of sphagnum moss

Set down in the scoured basins
Left by retreating glaciers),

Granite ledges
(The fog constant, edged with salt air).

We were to look for
Carnivorous plants, such as the sundew and pitcher plant,

The acidic, peat soil supports,
But saw none.

Blueberries thrived in the extreme nutrient-poor environment,
As did low heath shrubs, and moss—

Moss underfoot, on boulders, up the lengths of trunks and deadfall.
How quickly a moment is set adrift,

And memory (the imagination, that is)
Fills in with beachhead iris,

Marsh feltwort, and bird's-eye primrose;
Crowberry blue butterfly;

Deer-hair sedge, roseroot stonecrop, pearlwort;
Two kinds of dragonflies:

Forktails and spot-winged gliders;
Palm warblers, Lincoln's sparrows, boreal chickadees, and spruce
    grouse;

Dragon's mouth orchids,
Mountain cranberry, reindeer lichen,

Nova Scotia false foxgloves . . .
What we read ahead and after mixed up

With what we saw or hoped to see.
I recall

Spruce and fir and larch
And the ground slippery underfoot,

And somehow with each step
I managed to balance and move ahead and on.

ICEBERG IN MIST

Nothing much to see:
                            a white gessoed canvas,
A surface prepared but no mark acted upon it.

Ice cracks, echoes within fogbound space.
Ice groans. A slab calves with a splash.

To be *here* is to be remote:
                            apart from, astray.
Clouds shift and reveal a spectral range

Of white on white on white on white:
Blue under-glow like milk in a galvanized pail.

A MAP OF VENICE

The dark descends.
                Warm air shimmers
At the rendezvous we call the *horizon*.

The wind, what wind there is,
                          is hardly tangible:
A memory of silk pulled across
Pale skin where a pulse pulses.

How easily we forget the initial threshold,

Forget the tautly wound and elaborate distance
We navigated
               to arrive at the labyrinth's center.

A mirror empties itself each night.
Nonetheless,
              stars—spiked and bristly—float
Amid the canal's silvered mars and pewtered nicks.

SEEING THINGS

As if the perishable matter of dreams,
Snow crystalized out of the night sky.
Instead of falling, the snow seemed to rise,

To hover then rise: a star chart, yet random,
If by random we mean a pattern not yet
Fixed or determined, and the snow,

Which had been vapor condensing on dust
Just the moment before, *appeared* as if without order.
The dark, translucent mist—now edged,

Angled, hexagonal, frozen—trapped moonlight,
Meager given cloud cover and the pared-back phase,
Still light enough for us to behold the ephemeral.

THE VERNACULAR

The strangeness of beauty:
A raw clay scar
      Where an oak uprooted,

    Or a fiery knot
Of snakes coupling,
      Or power lines

    Slung with ice,
Or my sister, for instance—
      Backlit, silhouetted—

    At sunset
Waving away the camera.
      Not the moment before,

    Not the moment after:
A coincidence of light
      Fixed on film.

TO CONFIRM THE EARTH'S ROTATION

Days like drops of mercury merge,
The particular subsumed into the general,
And soon there is no unoccupied space.
The past, so it seems, vast, everlasting:
No room for attic, crawl space, or cellar,

Not to mention the junk we've gathered,
Imagining a beach house furnished one day,
Or selling the inherited antiques when
The economy turns around, demand returns.
How far away yesterday retreats, a frontier

Of fogs and icy rain, oddly out of fashion,
Quaint, devoid of nostalgia or ache.
We lived there once and have moved on,
We say. Yet there it is: impinging,
Invasive, like a vine you cut back each summer

That returns the next year more vigorous,
Tangled, determined, weighing down
The azaleas, the dogwood, the camellias,
The cultivated rough edge of the yard
Gone more rough, a realm of weeds

With which the vine will also have its way.
American English could use a word like
Whilst to capture the waylaid hurry that is
Today, now already headlong, relinquishing
The present tense to the past, the *is* to *was*,

The *will be* theorized, but only in books.
We will walk the broken trail up around

The headlands to watch the water's
Green translucence and bright froth unbraid,
And the sun, to confirm the earth's rotation,

Will hesitate and swell before it slips into the deep,
Or maybe it stalls there, hovers as if
To commemorate some rare solar effect—
Flares, dark spots, an aurora's array—
Those who came before knew enough to heed.

THREE MATHEW BRADY CIVIL WAR PHOTOGRAPHS

1. *CONFEDERATE DEAD BEHIND A STONE WALL*
AT FREDERICKSBURG, VIRGINIA

Where the glass negative broke:
    A silky, liquid black,
Like spilled scrivener's ink,
    Pools in the print's margin.

Mouth gone slack, eyes upward,
    Face glazed with blood, the man—
Lifeless, slumped, and tangled
    In a tarp—looks for God.

Two leafless trees hold up
    A scratched sky's leaden weight.
Autumn? Winter? No wind
    To sway the upright trees.

Such a long exposure
    To affix the fallen
(Staged or happened upon),
    Abandoned to this ditch.

2. WILDERNESS, NEAR CHANCELLORSVILLE, VIRGINIA

It is a slow process:
                    fallen and standing trees,
Propped, bent, a clutter of intersections—

All moss- and lichen-ridden,
                    woodpecker pecked,
Bored by grubs, antler-scraped, bark rubbed free—

Hard to tell from the decay
                    the living from the dead,
The dead from the almost dead—

A tree—
         horizontal across the creek,
Uprooted when a flash flood cut the cutbank—

Still leaves, blossoms, bears fruit.
                    Without a buttress,
A long dead sycamore remains upright.

3. BURYING THE CONFEDERATE DEAD AT FREDERICKSBURG, VIRGINIA

Jesus said, *Let the dead bury the dead.*

Two caskets and five or six canvas-
Covered bodies wait beside a trench
Three black men have spent all day digging.

Given their druthers, they'd obey scripture.

STUDY FOR "THE DAY OF JUDGMENT"

The risen let go of their grave clothes,
Their bodies, held down so long, now weightless,
Pale, unfamiliar, but bodies nonetheless,
Each an inadvertent spark, a fire-released seed:
Live embers lifted skyward on a thermal;

While below, devils drag the fallen deeper
Through vents and fissures, through bedrock,
Where dark divines a frozen dance,
A hoary latticework, an ice-embellished cage:
The least of their misfortunes unimaginable.

PEMAQUID POINT

Nothing comes clear. The surface—supple,
Mutable, unbroken—lifts, curves, and rocks,
Conceals a massive depth, a cobalt dark,

Like a covenant entered into that remains a mystery,
Even though submitted to, encompassed by.
The mindless motion, one could believe, embodies

Mindfulness. The sky tosses about in the lunge,
As gray as a cloud forest, as white as unraveled lace
Where a swell overcomes, submerges into,

Enlarges another—the motion constant, random,
Somehow predictable: a dance built upon a minimal
Lexicon of gestures with which one improvises.

Fog, a feature of morning, subsides, burns off,
As distance stretches beyond its confines.
The shallow blues are shadow upon translucency.

THE WAPSIPINICON
for Bob Crum

The surface, not overrun
With reflections, gives way
To an unobscured pebbled bed.

The river remains level, untroubled.
A sun-flash here and there
Suggests the water's swiftness.

Eight or nine sand grains,
Stirred up, swirl into an orbit,
Only to resettle a little downstream.

A water strider, held aloft,
Skims upon the moving transparency.
We haul our canoes up onto the sandbar,

Wait for the kindling to catch.
We cannot see the stars for all the daylight.

I . II . III . **IV.** V . VI . VII . VIII .

THE COMPLETE LIST OF EVERYTHING
(Recovered Loose-leaf Pages)

The elliptical grammar of grackles
Misdirection discontinuity
The wrong tool for tossing manure

The elsewhere silt erodes toward
A creature of habit
A narrow view between two houses

The river of forgetting a forgotten river
Steps in a liturgical dance
Ricochet of reflections

Dew on poppies and Ligurian grapes
Bruised bloom of a nocturne
Multiple itineraries

Telepathy premonition clairvoyance
Roots that penetrate the rocky substrate
Out of the gray vastness a whale's eye

Floating world
The contiguous path
The violent presence of angels

Inner ear unbroken line
Word meaning *grown accustomed to*
Snow on stepping stones

The washed-out vigil of noon
Transitivity fluency
Harsh terrain not mentioned on the map

A wind chime's four-note variations
Orchard of lightning
The palace at 4 a.m.

A hitherto purely imagined form
The precision of chance
Dossier emptied of evidence

Silvery floating web fragments called *Mary's yarn*
Ruin overrun by wildflowers and vines
Word meaning *to court chance*

Mortgage still owed on a burned building
Micrographia agrapha
Thorn that grew to be a spindle

The unspeakable spoken as paraphrase
Allegory's single-pulley ropework
Behind and ahead a narrowing road

The contagion's complex equation
Woody Guthrie singing "I Ain't Got No Home in This World
  Anymore"
Spinning firework called the "Catherine wheel"

The embraced contradictions
Dumb luck
The austerities of Minimalism

The Spell of the Falling Star
The Spell of the Swallow
Spider in a dumpling

Thaumatrope of a bird and cage
One who speaks quickly fearing interruption
The shush and lullaby of a broom

A tin weathercock
A preexisting condition
The error that confirms perfection

An object potent with magic
The soot-black cavity of a fireplace
Prow ornament

Curve of a boar's tusk
Nails of different calibers
Pins and needles a nettle

Pittura Metafisica
A glimpse of the infinite
A worthy heir a balancing act

A derelict raft's cargo of sand
A polymathic miscellany
Trout with mint and lemon

The annulled marriage
The error of enthusiasm
Son House singing "John the Revelator"

Soft target sod house soapsuds
The accused in the dock
Dog years a stitch in time

A whalebone slide rule
Spectra of nebulae
The rhyme of *spider* and *beside her*

Voices as in a fugue
Vocabulary flashcards
Detroit Chicago Chattanooga Baton Rouge

An audience with Death
A series of etudes
Lethean shallows a shoreless ocean

THE LAST SUNDAY IN LENT

In Sunday school, a girl watches the wind outside the windows inhabit the dark shape of pines. The girl considers the unsayable name of God. She, too, has a name no one has spoken or dares speak. Sometimes it is sweet on her tongue like hard candy. Sometimes it burns like an ember. She dips a slender paintbrush into a jar of water and writes—no one watches—her secret name in water on the linoleum floor. The other children practice signing as they sing "This Little Light of Mine." The girl watches the name evaporate, and thinks, *My light is not so little.*

ANOTHER READING

As her client, you are given the sturdiest wooden chair, the chair on which a hanged man once stood. You sit down on the scuff where his heel had kicked and skittered away the chair. She is a palmist and claims the lines on your hands read: *The marvelous is born from refusal.* Her shop looks out onto the stage of a piazza. It is Ash Wednesday. In drizzle, a carny stands, beside a collapsed canvas tent, as blue cotton candy melts down his forearm. You ask for another reading. *This time,* you say, *let me first take off my gloves.*

MELANCHOLIA

On the periodic table, it is the densest of elements. It does not refract or reflect, but absorbs all light. On the tongue, it has no taste at all. All day the rain falls in its room. All night the rain. Mold blackens the walls. Drops slip from the ceiling and, in a future not yet imaginable, stalactites and stalagmites begin to grow, barring the door, the windows. A poor cousin to gold and lead, it never quite sleeps, is never quite roused. It averts its eyes like a beggar. It broods on the dull edge of its brooding, on an arrival again postponed.

ARCADIAN INSCRIPTIONS

You write: *wind grafted to an apple tree*,
And offer no argument the image fulfills.
You write: *like an ember blown upon*
And think of wind grafted to an apple tree.
That is your first error.
Did you mean *inert* or *misbegotten*?
In the distance, a muted light grows a bit brighter:
An ember, blown upon, that soon fades.

PARABLE WITH MY FATHER AS A BOY

He woke at an hour the church bells no longer strike. At that porous border between night and morning, he gleaned windfall, russet to rose, all pocked and blemished, and pressed it to a winey, tin-edged cider. He foraged for seeds and nuts, dug up tubers. Hung the whitetail from the rafters and slit its throat; its blood ticktocked into a galvanized pail.

All this before his sisters woke and pestered him: *Why has the milk soured? Is that the Adversary stealing our nanny goat? Only yesterday, while you napped, he sowed tares in the field!*

The boy was abandoned, not raised, by wolves. For his first three years, he suckled what he could to get by: a fox, a star-nosed mole, a skunk, a nanny goat. As an adult, tossing back the last of a martini he would say, *Milk is for babies and barbarians.* To stay warm, the boy rubbed two sticks together. The boy rode an old broke-down mare to school through a blizzard. No saddle. No saddle blanket. He'd say, *A horse's heart is as blue as a glacier's.* From page four of his *Eclectic First Reader*, the boy read aloud to the empty schoolroom:

> *The two boys run fast.*
> *They run as fast as they can.*
> *One of the boys has no hat.*
> *Here is a small dog.*
> *He has the boy's hat.*
> *The boys cannot catch the dog.*

The boy read that once the universe fit into the space of a jelly jar. The hard part, he figured, was screwing on the lid. Nestled in the hayloft, the boy would listen to the night sounds: sleet in the branches, a distant church bell striking the hour, the wolves loping away from town on the highway's icy, gravelly shoulder. Before he falls asleep, the boy frets about the boy in the story, the one without a hat. *It is winter,* the boy thinks, *he'll catch his death of cold.*

MY FATHER AMID THE SHADES

He stands at the doorway, tired
Of the labyrinth's granite passages,
Lights another cigarette, coughs—

Younger now than I am, but worse
For wear. Twice split by stroke,
He has yet to relearn right-handedness

Or to speak with confidence without a slur.
His face is not his own and yet
I recognize him beneath his mask

That peels like the paper of a wasps' nest.
Like him, I neither fear nor serve
The gods, but by their favor I am allowed

This audience. My grief, once rage,
Is now more like the finest of splinters
That goes unnoticed as it works

Its way to the surface of the skin.
He does not recognize me—an old man
Among the shades—and why would he?

I am an interloper hoping to curry favor,
To have the past explained at last.
It would be easier to foretell the future.

A jostle of stars at the edge of the Crab Nebula pinpoints the heart of Taurus. Under the right conditions and with a steady hand, you can see it with binoculars. As with most things, the conditions are rarely right, the hand never steady enough.

Snow arrives on the hackles of wolves, but from where? As before the snow, one must see an image for what it is: fugitive, belated. Mute like a river. Like the stupor of smoke when a bell jar is placed over a lit candle. Like a snowflake caught on a sniper's eyelash as he aims.

No homespun melancholy, no traveler's nostalgia, this ennui works its way into the marrow, lodges there, and enters the blood. Thus infected, the chronic effects beginning to show, it is best not to enter the underworld, attempt to lure a shade out of the realm of shades.

All stories begin in the forest and only later do we move out of its dark to follow the herds, to build with mud and straw. A shimmer of stream through the woods is not enough to lure us back. We were happy: everything still to be done.

A snare of horsehair. Cinders on her cuffs. Blocked access to an exit. Borrowed time. Da Vinci's chapter called *How to Make an Imaginary Animal Look Natural*. Bronze boats afloat on a sea of rice. Spiral galaxy. The palpable pull of gravity.

Odysseus narrates three tales of forgetfulness. As he speaks, he tastes the lotus honey on his tongue, feels the burn of salt in his throat. He has no memory of the past, only memories of the stories he tells, memories of telling the stories.

A fogged-over pond floats above the thawed ground like a monocle. Blue heather and other ruderals take hold in burnt-out places. The viewer, absorbed in viewing, takes note of distortion at the periphery, how straight lines there ache toward curves.

There's no refusing the refuse, the detritus, the accumulations, the scrape of scrap crushed, trashed, deemed useless at last. Of all the subsets of the set of the whole, which is represented by the intersection labeled a? Vestiges corrode, cede to rust.

A day moon, silver damascened with iron, shimmers a little. The fields look like fields in a Book of Hours where magpies follow a sower. What he casts down the birds take up. He does not look back. He looks ahead. He is the sower.

A non-native invasive is introduced, or a horse is ridden into a funeral pyre, or you imagine a quantity where counting no longer makes sense, or Jesus, distracted, a little annoyed by their ploy, wastes their time, scrawls magic words in the dust.

Virga above a landscape made distance tactile. Then she spoke the truth. He wanted an explanation. She explained that there is no objectivity— how can one see without the interference of interpretation? He recalled her hesitations, not the words she uttered.

My brother strikes the door slammed on him. To enhance this charm of anger, my brother strikes again the door slammed on him. Not to knock, but to knock it down, break and enter. All he finds inside are swept floors, open cabinets, and empty drawers.

The day the war ends, one notes the lazy way smoke hoists itself up out of the chimneys, how the last of the migrating flocks, drawn elsewhere, spills out of the trees. Some things are known only in transit. One weeps, thus fails to behold the soul exit its body.

What is Italian for *its paltry semblance*, for *the birth of specters and phantoms?* The bird, and not the birdcall, is hidden. While you decide on your order, the waiter caresses the rumpled tablecloth smooth. Each item on the menu has a red line drawn through it.

How does amber preserve a sliver of Baltic light? What is allowed the rose, burdened as it is with significance, its innermost aspects threadbare, worse for wear? Have you, like I, at last been thwarted by the vagaries of circumstances?

Not a single name in the hotel registry. The cage of the elevator waits at an upper floor. The clerk and concierge, you assume, have stepped away for a moment. The buzz of overhead lights evens out the silence. The little bell waits: polished, unrung.

Like the plump bee on the hollyhock, or the garter snake sunning on slate, one is merely a lodger here. Swifts trace elaborate spirals above a ruined chapel with four winds as walls. A muddy wheel rut, full of last night's rain, gleams.

A lead plumb holds the vertical. The alchemical glyph for *lead* is the scythe of Saturn. Saturn's heart, cut into, gleams a moment like lead. It, as well, is sweet touched to the tongue. On the periodic table, lead is the last of the stable elements.

The hiss and crack of quick-burning tinder. The piano and its cabinet of hammers. The sound of a mountain waterfall through dense forest. A leather bellows's asthmatic huff. A sudden clatter outside like an avalanche of axes.

"Surely, a time will come when on those frontiers, a farmer, as he ploughs with his curved blade, will turn up ancient javelins eaten away with flaky rust, or will strike with his heavy hoe empty helmets, and marvel at giants' bones in the upturned graves."

How does the nightingale extricate itself from night? What is the word that means *that which could not have been conceived of at the outset*? Why did she smile when we called her honesty *ruthless*? How does the green shoot break through the bark inaudibly?

Like the candle a midwife bears at a tragedy's end. Like sparrows all winter weaving shrouds. Like the bloat and draggle of a body caught in a deluge. Like the tarnished tin of a stagnant pool. Like a pack of jackals asleep among the tombs.

River mist lifts in the middle distance and the bridge beyond, foundered in fog, submerges into background. How else to read the bluish gray expanse across a deeper bone-soot gray, the arcana of crosshatches, smudges, and ink smears?

The lodger, lost, consults the logic of the ant's seemingly aimless to and fro. On his face, moonlight falls, fits as easily as a death mask. The fire sings from its ring of rocks. Wind hews the drifts of grit. The lodger wears an open wound called *brevity*.

TROUBLE IN MIND

An overlay of shadows and shade. Crows in the winter corn. The goldenrod flame-like. The body of Jesus translated into the body of Christ. The lid of the Shaker box fits so snugly that when it's replaced, the air inside sighs. The net floats like a cloud, the skein's interstices: bright points. A sea of negative space. She was a beautiful girl. From the depths of the pinewood, how does one imagine the idea of *a clearing*? Always a swarm of images at hand waiting to inhabit the framed mirror. By *poverty*, I meant the poverty of language. You thought it all so Romantic: the craggy knolls, the tumbledown shacks, and bosky hillsides. At the party, one entertains doubts. Did you say *a cursory personality* or *a personal curiosity*? Did she ask *how to avoid the void?* In a single day: a retrospective of weathers. The hanged man afloat between two worlds. I have spent my life contemplating the play of light upon an interior: the complexity of perception, the perception of complexity. You watch a thought transmute into a *thought of watching a thought*. Tugged at, a circle expands to an ellipse. A marriage of dusk light and pearl. A plate of cherries to feed those in a lifeboat. A thousand ooliths. *She was a beautiful girl and,* she said, *that's where her trouble started.*

THE SIDE EFFECTS OF MIMICRY

What can be said of the somber boulevard
Of pollarded trees, all elbows and knuckles?
Or, for that matter, the right-angled
Geometry of the houses? The cyclical return to realism?
How can one capture the underlying melancholy
Of mimicry, without specific reference to it?
Above it all, in the upper right-hand corner,
A milky passage of blue to suggest *sky*.
Although cancelled on the calendar with an *X*,
The day, continuing with its inevitable logic,
Bristles like the rich burr of a drypoint line.
The trees seem victims of a methodical violence.
Wind moves in and around them, but the trees do not move.

I . II . III . IV . V . **VI .** VII . VIII .

THE INTERVENING YEARS

The ridge is lacelike, stone woven of fog,
Strata uplifted, aslant, eroded, broken.
Rags of mists drag. Clouds submerge the peak.
After a good long while a swift river
Brings down a mountain to its valley.
Until then, the sublime proportion of *until then*.
Halfway up the mountain the road ends.

LINES AT MIDSUMMER

A wall crumbles.
               A salamander maps the rearranged rocks,
The ivy-loosened mortar, the moss-cool niches.

As an ideogram follows an ink-dipped brush,
                                      one meditates briefly
On the brevity of things.

THE ATTENTION AN ENIGMA DEMANDS

They drove up and round the mountains
But did not find the alpine lake
So full of sky one might mistake it for sky.
When embers fly up and draw one's eyes
To stars, distance has little to do with
How one thing is like another.

ELSEWHERE

On the mountain top:
Blue gentians,

Shadowed shallows
Of snow at midsummer.

Halfway down,
A suspended waterfall:

A braid and rush,
Its taut end

Never loosening,
Its frayed end

All frazzle and unravel.
Water rushes,

Zigzags down
To a high meadow,

Plumps up
The rough grass

Grazing horses
Feed upon.

The road ends.
To go anywhere

One must backtrack,
Find a way

Around the mountain.
The air, transparent,

Holds a chill
At this altitude.

We stay awhile,
Lean on a fence,

Hope the horses
Look up, come near.

Their attention is elsewhere
As it should be.

But we attend
To looking as we do,

Believing the visible
Opens onto

The almost invisible,
That which we seek.

We are passersby.
The horses know it

And keep at their business—
Shooing flies

With articulate tails,
Moving ahead

A step at a time
Through summer grasses.

MEDITATION AT RIO DEVA

How to distinguish a trick
Of the eye
From wind in a chestnut?

All knowledge
Is arcane
And thus prevents

Easy access
To the immanent beyond.
It's hard to get used to.

As when detained
By a fleeting thought,
You see the sun emerge

From clouds
Like a dew-wet fox
From underbrush

And only now
Recollect the overcast,
The gloomy humidity,

The winding road
Through tunnels
And forest

That left you here.
Water eddies and rushes
And some unseen blossoming

Offers an unheard-of
Sweetness
Without cloy,

Sharp-edged citrus
Mixed with cold
Spray from the rapids.

The river continues
Like the thread of a story,
Spun out.

An ordinary story.
Slips and lapses
Where you expect them.

To look back
(Who cannot look back?)
Is an act of revision.

In the mountains,
You think of the forces
Behind form:

The buildup,
The long wearing down.
Scree clatter.

The riverbank lined
With flattened oval
Palm-sized stones.

The mountain unmoved.
The mountain transient
In a summer of rains,

Rain like an accusation,
Daily rain the mountain sheds
And the river conveys:

A legible serpentine script
Through what erodes,
Around what remains.

SOJOURN AND TRANSIT

On a mountain girdled by light-flecked streams,
We walk a path threaded through woods. The river

Below still high at midsummer.
When clouds cover the sun, the air ambers.

Red-billed choughs ride the ridge edge on updrafts.

What is doubt made of that it casts a shadow,
Even at noon? Rapids rush as spray and rainbow

Around boulders. Nothing, not even memory,
To distract us from the quickened austerity of noon,

From the water's headlong lexicon of vowels.

After a lunch of local bread and sharp-edged blue cheese,
We'll descend the dark of a Paleolithic cave,

Transit a distance of thirty thousand years.
Until then, a laze and slur of afternoon light cools and dapples

The limestone slab on which we recline.

IN THE PRESENCE OF ANIMALS

We descend
Into the dank dark
    To behold bison,

    Stags, and ponies;
Crushed ochre
    Mixed with tallow;

    A burnt willow twig's
Charcoal reanimated
    By flashlight

    And try not to ascribe
A liturgical drama
    Upon the space—

    Penumbral, hidden,
Preserved,
    Despite the years' accretions—

    And yet we feel
The presence of the sacred,
    Venerate

    The slow progress
Of herds
    Across cave walls,

    The patience
Of a maker making marks.
    The bison, head down,

Consults the new grass.
An agitated horse
        Bridles.

A MAP OF THE FRONTIER

Far off, cicadas start.
Dust follows a horse
To a grassy patch.

The day is an entrance.
The day entrances.
To find the granary,

Follow the mice and sparrows.
The day moon goes its way,
The clouds the other

And thereafter are forgotten.
To find the mice and sparrows,
Follow the hawk.

AS THROUGH A SHEER CURTAIN

Heat haze far away:

What seems immeasurable vastness
Is but an hour's walk at most,

Opening there to other distances.
Perhaps the river meanders

Like a snake scaled in sun glints,
Or maybe the forest

Comes down to the slow water's edge,
Conceals it in cool shade

So that trout gather
Beneath a ragged jam

Of leaves, sticks, and branches.
But what one sees

Is faraway
As in a dream:

A landscape as through a sheer curtain
Where the indistinct edges of things

Smudge, shift, and bray.

SOUVENIRS

The sky, on permanent display,
Offers a single cloud,
A crisscross of contrails.

                                  In scraggly
Upland trees, in grasses,
Sunlight transfigures to sugar.

A nursing mare shivers
Away flies,
                shifts her weight
From one hoof to another.

Little rain puddles
Offer fragments of sky
Back to the sky.

                     We came
To find knapped flint
And arrowheads, but watch instead
The fed foal frolic.

I.II.III.IV.V.VI.**VII.**VIII.

THE COMPLETE LIST OF EVERYTHING
(An Addendum)

Candle in a still life snuffed out
A coal-hard luster a stone-skittered surface
Coda postscript afterword errata

The rough edge of a blueberry's sweetness
Not the pearl but the initial irritant therein
Half moon beneath the shelter of a bridge

Nameless shape a flock of starlings enacts
Consecrated relics blackboard drawings
Frontier for which a war is waged

The usual gossip the Gospel of Thomas
Chuck Berry singing "Memphis, Tennessee"
Mica flakes a ghost's vapor viscera

A waxy bit of lipstick smudged on her tooth
Chipped white paint on a tin-plated first aid kit
The erotics of a chocolate grinder

A summons a writ a warrant a subpoena
The cardsharp the trickster the hawker
Raw observations modest earnings

The worked gold leaf of an icon's halo
Façade chipped by bullets back to brick
The uncorrected error the damaged link

The litany of mile markers across the prairie
The fifth foreclosure on the block
Frugal savings speed trap double negative

Vein of talc through serpentine
Myrtle wreath tilted cradle chain reaction
Venetian footbridge April eclipse

Another infinity behind each decimal point
Time's constancy the accorded duration
A door removed and set on two sawhorses

Robert Johnson singing "Come On In My Kitchen"
Four cloaked mirrors a scruple of gold
Ocean surface desert floor nighttime sky

What Wallace Stevens calls *the vulgate of experience*
What flatters an evil spirit what enchants a fool
The intricate yet incomplete history of Hermeticism

A snake's ability to shed its skin
A plow's song a Mayan flint blade
Confirmed incidences of supernatural events

Wine lees roasted to produce a suitable black pigment
Splinters of pitch pine
Figures types and analogies

Tomatoes tied to stakes with torn stockings
A struck match's brevity the laze and loiter of clouds
Orion's belt raccoon scat beaver-felt hat

A plaster crack's zigzag a decline of scree
The Blue Ridge Skating Rink
One of ambiguity's several effects

Wattle and daub tongue and groove
Magic knots charms and incantations
Flock of sheep under a child's sway

The past like a mooring pole
Creek ice cracked with tossed rocks
Aqueducts wells and cisterns

Timbers felled in early autumn
Babylonian tablet snowmelt dwarf planet
A mishap of little consequence

A loss for words offshore accounts
The darkroom's burnt-out bulb
Memories unsullied so far

Thoth incarnated as an ibis
Plausible deniability glyphs and graphs
Slender means peonies eradicated disease

Bitter wind through a cedar blown
In a shepherd's cave a dug-out firepit
Light distorted by gravity's lens

What lingers of the ephemeral
The nothing-to-add the right-of-way
The angle of repose an angel's intercession

Olive orchard ablaze the bulldozed house
What the tide disinters daily
Noun meaning *time it takes a wound to heal*

Swift and tragic turn of events
A sloppy barroom kiss
Raw scold of Wichita wind

Beached whale towed out to sea
Drawn lots open season many mansions
Dionysus cloaked in goatskins

Ecclesiastes chapter 9 verse 1
Bob Dylan singing "Trying to Get to Heaven"
A door about to close

I.II.III.IV.V.VI.VII.**VIII.**

THE CONTINUOUS PRESENT

From a certain height and distance,
He can observe a river's meander,
How it turns back on itself
To move ahead
Toward some unseen body
Of water that pulls it, calls to it.
And on summer nights,
He can watch the ether propagate stars—
The orbs filled
With a glassblower's breath—
And with each new star
He must reconfigure the sight lines,
The map of the simple path home.
What is a body but the remnants of touch,
Marks left by previous contact
And collisions?
For a long time he believed
Looking down at a body of water
Or keeping current a ledger of stars
Was an antidote to uncertainty,
And not, as he knows now, a giving in
To it. He blinks and disrupts
The continuous present.
He pulls the car over
On the off-ramp's downward curve
And rolls down the window.
He cannot hear the water
Through the scrubby woodland,
Nor see the stars
Through the hazy dome of city light.
He listens to the traffic,

A rush this way and that,
As if any direction could be his destination,
A road that connects to a road home.

ABOVE AT AND JUST BELOW SEA LEVEL

On highest ground:
A hardwood hammock
Of mahogany, gumbo-limbo,
And strangler fig.

Each thought abstracted
Into language *is*.

Words turn easily to song
Pine bromeliad, wild cinnamon,
Poisonwood,

Shoal grass, manatee grass, turtle grass,

Ghost crab . . .

Out of a murky broth:
Mangrove roots.

DIVINATION BENEATH THUNDER

Detritus in the swash zone.
A tangled ball of trap line.
A bull's horn acacia thorn.

Jettisoned dunnage
That once served
As skids and blocks.

A lobster trap float.
Sea glass among the shell hash.
The left hand of a pair

Of latex shrimp-heading gloves.
A sand-scratched, deflated Mylar balloon.
An old teak rudder.

A mermaid's purse bundle.
A beholder assumes
The meaningfulness of space

Between and among these objects,
Cast after all at random:
A future there to be read.

PLAIN SIGHT

The moment, marooned with its shadow,
Is viewed one frame at a time,
But the sequence of events,
The implied continuity, is no less sure,
What with the glitches and slippages,
The still point blurred by a bad splice,
The uneven terrain that is memory.

The horizon soldered with gold
Is a mere embellishment of happenstance.
In the Key West Cemetery,
In the shade of an aboveground vault,
A red hen pecks among the gravel.
Somewhere a rooster crows,
Crows again as if unheard, unheeded.

Little sliver of moon. The sky powdered graphite.
Late dark not black but tarnished silver.
Abstract effects on a figurative ground.
As a starting point: a coordinate grid,
Stars and more stars, a shiver and flicker
Of points set down along intersections of x and y.
Boats bob and nod. Each mast describes an arc.

Clouds disperse and regenerate,
And out of emptiness: change and emptiness.
Field notes are kept, yet so little is set down.
The underside of some clouds: storm-dark,
Inky like an overexposed negative.
Each brush-mark delible, wiped away in time
With subsequent turpentine washes.

In the distance, lines dissolve.
The foreground is unruly with detail.
The specter of disorder translates into order,
Or at least as an orderly and ghostly form.
In plain sight, a dragonfly hovers.
A scorpion skitters from a sidewalk crack—
Alarmed, armed as it makes a retreat.

IN THE EVER-FRESHENED KEYS

Shadow movements regulate
The length of the day's hours.

A hollow lotus pod rocks,
Harnesses what breeze there is.

This garden is a garden on a map
Of paradise woven into a prayer rug.

A green canopy and tropical sun
Hide the celestial movements,

The quantum entanglements,
The ever-present disturbing beauty

From which the discreet modeling
Of shadow has distracted us for now.

ALL SHALL BE RESTORED
for Lisa Weiss

The map's edge implies
A realm beyond it,

Perhaps the unbearable
Proximity of the divine.

What is that blank region
Called between *far* and *near*?

We live in the conditional,
Await transfer across the interim.

The sun, half aloft, half submerged,
Is like a child's drawing of the sun.

Time slows and wobbles
Like a bullet through gelatin.

The coordinates are superimposed
Over an arc of violet sky.

From the present, we hew
Toward a violet future.

The day is a sheaf of drawings.
The day is a notebook's privacies.

Two vertical monoliths
Uphold a horizontal third.

A seagrass meadow
Circles the patch reef,

A greenish stain
Beneath the surface blues.

The flame halo of reentry
Is not caused by friction,

But by the compression of air
In front of the falling object.

Through an anomaly of memory
The present tense is recalled;

And I feel like I've been here before
Feel like I've been here before

A ghost grid floats on the surface,
An abandoned net full of holes.

In the offing, a red hull bobs:
A splintered wreck, a derelict.

At the heart of the square
A point is placed,

Once conjoined,
Twin rivers bypass each other.

One can imagine the parallel lines
Continuing on forever.

For now, each hovers above the other:
Held steady, held apart.

A body of water. A bay.
A nest of smaller islands.

Where the earth curves
Away, boats disappear.

To draw the surface,
Practice the lowercase cursive *l*.

Let the linked loops
Pile up as a litany of waves.

To stay cool we follow
The fort's shaded arcade of archways.

Spiral stairs lead up
To an overview of the island.

Each creek, stream, and river
Forgotten; the rain itself forgotten.

Beyond the shallows and shoals:
An elegant austerity of seas.

SANCTUARY

I am familiar with the impurity of recollection, the errors in continuity, the fleeting glimpse easily claimed as witness, the kind of ill-lit moment a photograph might hoard. I live, as you do, between contingency and control, between presence and distance. Let's call this *the year a child washed up on shore.* You saw the image as I did, repeatedly on the news and in the paper, the little one face down on the waterline's saturated sand. Yet nothing disturbed the moth's reign over the night. Nothing healed the tree peppered with hundreds of weeping woodpecker holes. Nothing bleached out a dye of turmeric and iron oxide. In the Bible there are two parallel narratives of mass infanticide. The first foretelling the second. The second recalling the first. The child does not writhe or jerk. The child does not shiver beneath its wet clothes. The child, held still in an extended moment of composed stillness, is dead.

OWL OF MINERVA

Threat of rain all day, but no rain.
Ripe green lanterns weigh down the fig tree.
At twilight, one hears but does not see the wasps.

Like a sheet of paper curling back on itself as it burns,
A storm cloud's dark edges turn inside out to darker.

Although the rain's begun, a jackdaw flies
Back and forth, agitated between twin pines.
All night the owl whose call you did not heed.

DEBRIS OF AN OCTOBER EVENING

The cloudy gray of a night
Reveals a trace we call *the past:*

Its ineluctable opulence—
The duration of an afterimage—
Is unaskewed or patinaed by distance.

Memory emerges from the periphery,
Spreads like spilled ink on a blotter.

At midnight, a cock calls out alarm.

Iguanas roost in trees.

DREAM TRANSLATION
for Jay Wright

Out of fog, a narrow house coalesces,
Gravity superseded as it floats aloft.

Memory: permeable, easily stained.
Beneath the tap a glass vase fills:

Its oboe note changes as water rises.
Wind rifles through the shotgun house

In the front door and out the back
As a block of light inches up the wall.

Not a shotgun house, Jay says, *but a* shogon house,
Which is to say, the house of God.

ACKNOWLEDGMENTS

Sincere thanks to the editors of the following journals who first offered these poems, often in earlier drafts, a home:

|Adroit Jounal:
My Father Amid the Shades

American Journal of Poetry:
The Attention an Enigma Demands
The Intervening Years
Lines at Midsummer
Souvenirs

Booth:
As Through a Sheer Curtain

Cimarron Review:
Another Reading

Cincinnati Review:
Iceberg in Mist

Colorado Review:
The Complete List of Everything (*An Addendum*)

Copper Nickel:
To Confirm the Earth's Rotation

Crazyhorse:
The Complete List of Everything (*Recovered Loose-leaf Pages*)

december:
Cold Mountain

Diode:
Arcadian Inscriptions
In the Presence of Animals
The Wapsipinicon

Elsewhere:
A Public Education

Flexible Persona:
Plain Sight

Harvard Review:
All Shall Be Restored

Hollins Critic:
Dream Translation

Hotel Amerika:
Thinking about the Afterlife

Kenyon Review:
A Map of Venice

Newfound:
The Continuous Present

New World Writing:
Parable of My Father as a Boy
Meditation at Rio Deva

Ocean State Review:
Spell for Calling Down Rain
Study for "The Day of Judgment"

Plume:
Book of Hours
The Complete List of Everything (*An Excerpt*)
Melancholia
Trouble in Mind

poets.org:
Three Mathew Brady Civil War Photographs

Rock and Sling:
Elsewhere
Owl of Minerva

Sou'wester:
Divination beneath Thunder

Talking River:
In the Ever-Freshened Keys
Debris of an October Evening

Tupelo Quarterly:
The Side Effects of Mimicry

Two Hawks Quarterly:
Fever Dream

UCity Review:
The Vernacular

Wildness:
The Last Sunday in Lent

I want to thank the good people at The Studios in Key West, for a residency where many of these poems were first drafted, and to offer my gratitude to Gabrielle Teschner and Lisa Weiss, two visual artists in residency with me at the time, for their generous kindness, good conversation, and inspiring company.

Love and deep appreciation to Jennifer Atkinson who read and commented on many versions of each of these poems along the way.

NOTES

The National Archives and the Academy of American Poets jointly commissioned the poem "Three Mathew Brady Civil War Photographs."

In "The Set of the Whole," the line and a half "A coherent totality of meaning from odds / And ends" quotes Claire Preston's *Sir Thomas Browne and the Writing of Early Modern Science.*

"Thinking about the Afterlife" quotes the chorus of the Christian hymn "In the Sweet By-and-By," by Sanford Fillmore Bennett and Joseph P. Webster.

"A Public Education" quotes *McGuffey's First Eclectic Reader.*

The quoted passage in "Book of Hours" is from Virgil's *Georgics.*

"All Shall Be Restored" quotes "Déjà Vu" by David Crosby.

The three poems titled "The Complete List of Everything" sample from many sources. Borrowed language (and much that is not) is italicized. The idea of a "complete list of everything" comes from Richard Wilbur's wonderful 1966 essay "Poetry and Happiness."

Rachel Eliza Griffiths

ERIC PANKEY is the author of thirteen books of poetry. His poetry, essays, and reviews have appeared widely in such journals as the *Iowa Review*, the *New Yorker*, and the *Kenyon Review*. He is a professor of English and the Heritage Chair in Writing at George Mason University. He currently resides in Fairfax, Virginia.

milkweed
editions

Founded as a nonprofit organization in 1980, Milkweed Editions is an independent publisher. Our mission is to identify, nurture and publish transformative literature, and build an engaged community around it.

milkweed.org

Interior design by Mary Austin Speaker
Typeset in Bulmer MT

Bulmer is a late transitional typeface designed by punchcutter
William Martin in the late eighteenth century to print the
Boydell Shakespeare folio edition. Described as "both delicate
and spirited, thoroughly English" by the typographical
historian D. B. Updike, Bulmer offers higher contrast than its
predecessors, and flourished serifs on the uppercase R and
Q. The digital version of Bulmer is based upon the foundry
version of the typeface, which was designed by Morris Fuller
Benton in 1923 for Monotype Imaging.